M000011717

Flying Airplanes:
for Fun *and* Money!

(A practical guide to becoming a
Professional Pilot)

By Nathaniel E. Erman

Flying Airplanes: for Fun *and* Money!
(A Practical Guide to Becoming a Professional Pilot)
Nathaniel E. Erman
Cover Art and Design by Koji Minami
Copyright © 2009 by Nathaniel E. Erman
First Printing 2009

Printed in the United States of America
Published by HEFF Publishing

All rights reserved. No part of this book may be reproduced or transmitted in any form or by any means, electronic or mechanical, including photocopying, recording, or by any information storage and retrieval system without written permission from the author and/or by the publisher.

Library of Congress Catalog Card Number: 2009933451

ISBN 978-0-578-03438-6

Disclaimer:
Although the author and publisher have made every effort to ensure the accuracy of information contained in this book, they do not assume and hereby disclaim any liability to any party for any loss or damage caused by the information, or lack thereof, contained within.

This book is a general information book which contains the opinions of the author. It is understood that the information contained in this book does not guarantee success of any kind. The reader accepts complete responsibility for any and all decisions and/or actions taken, caused or alleged to be caused directly or indirectly by the information and/or opinions contained in this book.

TABLE OF CONTENTS

- INTRODUCTION -

"Son, you're going to have to make up your mind about
growing up and becoming a pilot. You can't do both."
-Unknown

There are two kinds of pilots in the world: those who fly simply
for the joy and challenge of it, and those who do it for a living.
This book was written as a guide for the latter. Becoming a
professional pilot, while exhilarating and rewarding, is an
extremely difficult and costly experience both in time and
money. This guide was written for the aspiring professional
pilot, with the hope of helping to counsel and direct the process.
Through this book, it is my desire to impart some of my own
hard-earned knowledge, and in the process, alleviate some of
the difficulties you will encounter in becoming a professional
aviator.

With that in mind, it is important to note that the career path on
which you are embarking will still be difficult. Regardless of
my best intentions with this guide, your career pursuit will cost
you significant amounts of time, money, and most of all: effort.

You will have to work hard for this career, and it will not be as easy as you think it will be. At some point you will have a nervous breakdown, and will probably cry yourself to sleep out of frustration. Your flight training will undoubtedly take longer than you want, and it will cost more than you thought it would. You will fail check-rides, you will lose sleep, you will stress-out, and you will perspire. You will probably have a horrible first job, and will be furloughed from your second. But here's the good news: you will have more fun than you ever imagined. You will be proud of yourself and others will look up to you for your accomplishments. You will see the world from an office with a constantly changing view, and your experiences will topple those of most people you will meet.

Still interested? I certainly hope so, because the following pages will help you accomplish the job of your dreams. They were written as a common-sense guide, based on many years of real experience. Each chapter contains practical, goal-oriented advice, compiled from my own experiences, as well as those of my peers. Best of luck to you in your pursuit of professional aviation, I hope this guide will help you through the process.

See you in the air!

- GETTING STARTED -

The following topics are areas of general advice, which don't warrant entire chapters devoted to them. Nonetheless, these are topics of tremendous importance. It is my recommendation that you give genuine consideration to the following:

Mentors

Find a good mentor to help you through the process of becoming a professional pilot. This is a tool that is crucial to your success. Perhaps you have a family friend or an acquaintance who is either a professional or experienced pilot (hopefully both), from whom you can ask questions and advice of. Even if it is someone you do not personally know, don't make the mistake of being too shy to get their phone number or email address. Ninety-nine percent of the pilots I know would bend over backwards to help someone else in their aviation career. Just try! What do you have to lose?

Medical Certificate

All pilots are required to have a medical certificate that accompanies their pilot's license. There are three different levels, otherwise known as "classes", of medical certification. They are: first, second, and third classes. As a student pilot, you will be required to hold at least a third class medical certificate, which will also act as your Student Pilot's license. It is my sincere recommendation however, that you attempt the *first* class medical right away, before you take any lessons. Professional pilots are required to have at least a second class medical, but in most cases, a first class is required. By getting your first class medical examination right away, you will be able to immediately identify any medical issues you may have that would prevent you from maintaining a first class medical. It is better to find this information out now, than to realize it thousands of dollars and years of training later.

Medical certificates can be obtained from any Aeromedical Examiner (AME). A listing of AMEs in your area can be found at the following web address:
http://www.faa.gov/pilots/amelocator/

Money

"Forget all that stuff about lift, gravity, thrust and drag. An airplane flies because of money. If God had meant man to fly, He'd have given him more money."

-Unknown

Hopefully by now you have realized the financial commitment you are making in becoming a professional pilot. Airplanes are particularly expensive, both to buy and to maintain. Therefore, they are *very* expensive to rent. Airplanes also burn *a lot* of fuel. It is common to spend as much as $50-$60,000 to obtain the necessary ratings to land (no pun intended) your first job. But, it is money well invested if you are serious.

This guide will periodically discuss financial options and ways to save money on your flight training, but you need to be committed. If you don't have the money up front, there are ways to finance your training. Sally Mae is one of the most common career financing institutions around. Check them out at www.salliemae.com. In addition, many flight schools will work with their students on a payment plan. The point is this: if your dream is to pursue becoming a professional pilot, then don't let the money get in your way. There are ways to pay for it, and I guarantee you that people less fortunate than yourself have done it before. Besides, your first year as an airline pilot will more than pay for it... (yeah right!)

For those of you who have the means, here is what I recommend: Are you ready for this?

Buy an airplane.

You're probably in shock; however a lot can be said for this. Without going into too much detail, it will be cheaper for you in the end, and here's why:

1. Airplane rental fees are typically calculated at twice the actual operating cost of the aircraft, plus fuel.
2. You won't pay tax on rental fees.
3. Aircraft generally do not depreciate with time (i.e. you will get your investment back—and probably more).
4. There are enormous tax incentives to owning an airplane, particularly if you are a business owner.
5. You can purchase a *sufficient* airplane for the price of a new car.

So, if you are fortunate enough to buy your own aircraft, good for you. At a minimum it should help you invest in your training a bit more. I hope you do it. That said, this guide will progress in a cost-effective approach, which applies to aircraft renters and owners alike.

Time

Now that we're done talking about money, let's talk about time—because time is money, right? Arguable in life, but in aviation it's a proof-positive fact. The longer your training takes the more money you will spend. The longer you take to get to your dream job of being a professional pilot, the less you will make in salary over time. Time is money in aviation—always. Remember that.

Ideally you will commit your time to your training. When I was a flight instructor, the best students I had were not necessarily the smart ones or those who studied a lot. They were the students that came for lessons at *least* two or three times a week and who generally spent a lot of time at the airport. Three - five lessons per week is optimal. Any more than that is probably information overload, and I would not recommend it. If you can make the commitment to immerse yourself in your training, I guarantee it will save you substantial amounts of money and you will be closer to realizing your dream.

Unfortunately, not everyone can make this kind of time commitment, and that is understandable. If you fall into this category, then do as much as you can and devote as much time as possible to studying at home. The point is to immerse yourself in aviation. This is critical to your success and the more you do it, the better your chances of succeeding. I also recommend trying to get an aviation related job, such as a front desk position at the flight school or working the fuel truck for the airport—even if only part-time. This will further your aviation immersion, as well as help you build contacts who will undoubtedly help you along in your career. It also builds experience for your resume!

Flight Schools

This is imperative: don't underestimate the importance of finding the right flight school. There are a lot of options out there, and they'll all take your business, so you need to find the right one. Here is a categorization of your options:

1. Part 61 flight school

    This is the mom and pop type business. Most flight schools are part 61. It is your run-of-the-mill operation.

2. Part 141 flight school

    This may also be your standard local flight school, but what makes them different is that they are an accredited school. This should mean nothing to you unless you are getting college credit for your flying lessons, or you are paying for them through programs such as the GI Bill. In that case, part 141 should mean everything to you.

3. The College or University program

    Quite a few universities are offering flight programs that are typically attached to a formal degree of some sort, and are therefore Part 141 certified. Going this route depends on a lot of factors; however, I do recommend it if you are able. While it typically costs more and can certainly take more time, the knowledge base and skill set it leaves you with are exceptional. That said, having an aviation degree is usually not necessary when applying for pilot jobs, but you should be a college graduate if you want to progress in the field.

4. Aviation Academy

    These schools claim to take you from zero to airline
    pilot very quickly and with minimal flight time. They
    can supposedly do this because of their relationships
    with airlines. I recommend avoiding these schools like
    the plague. Going through their program does not in any
    way guarantee you an airline pilot job—an interview
    maybe, but not a job—and they will certainly cost you
    substantially more money. In fact, I personally know
    airline interviewers that shy away from hiring pilots
    from these programs because of their lack and quality of
    experience. You just don't need this. Enough said.

Once you have made your decision on the type of flight school
you will attend, begin looking at your options. I recommend
making an appointment with the chief flight instructor to ask
questions and get their literature. You may even consider taking
an introductory flight, which is like a flight school test-drive,
and is usually offered at a reasonably reduced price. The
following are some very important things to keep in mind when
selecting a flight school and you should certainly ask questions
regarding them when you visit:

- Availability of flight instructors –
  I'll elaborate on flight instructors a little later on, but make sure that the school has a flight instructor who will work with your schedule and desired time-line.

- Aircraft types and pricing –
  Initially I recommend using the cheapest airplane with an engine and two wings that you can find. You DO NOT need the brand new Cirrus with fancy avionics or a complex, high-performance aircraft—you'll have plenty of time for that later. Don't be talked into it either. You want to look for small, fuel-efficient airplanes with very simple avionics. If you can, get your training in what is called a "tail-wheel" aircraft, even if it costs slightly more. I'll explain why in subsequent chapters.

- Aircraft availability –
  Make sure that the flight school has enough airplanes to ensure that one will be available when you need it. If a flight school has only one or two aircraft, you run the risk of one or both going down for maintenance for long periods of time. On the other hand, a school may have lots of airplanes, but far too many renters or students monopolizing them.

- Maintenance of aircraft –

  This is not something to be too concerned with, as all flight schools are held to the same standard by the FAA, but I recommend asking anyhow. It's good to know whether they do their own maintenance or if it is contracted-out. Typically if a school has their own maintenance, even minor mechanical discrepancies will get fixed quicker, which is nice.

- Airport type –

  There are busy airports and slow ones, airports with towers and those without. All airports have their own make-up. Assuming you have options, I would recommend finding a slow airport that is controlled by a tower. This will give you the invaluable experience of dealing with air-traffic control, while not having to cope with busy airspace, which saves both time and money.

Flight Instructors

Almost equally as important as finding the right flight school is locating the right instructor within that school. A flight instructor is formally known as a CFI (Certified Flight Instructor), and there are different levels of certification for them. A CFI may instruct toward the Private and Commercial Pilot certifications. To give instruction towards the Instrument rating, a CFI must have obtained their CFII (Instrument Instructor). Likewise, to instruct towards a Multi-Engine rating the instructor must be an MEI (Multi-Engine Instructor). For your initial training, you will only need an instructor who is a CFI.

While all flight instructors are held to the same standard, they will all have different teaching styles and different levels of experience. Although counter-intuitive, I would be cautious in choosing the most senior instructor at the school—assuming you have been given a choice. Flight instruction tends to be a stressful job that is very transient in nature. The more senior instructors often tend to be burned-out and chomping at the bit to get a different job. The newer instructors, while relatively inexperienced, tend to have a lot more enthusiasm and are perfectly qualified—they wouldn't be there otherwise. The instructor I recommend the most is the part-timer. Part-time flight instructors are usually not doing it because they need the money or flight time, but because they really enjoy it. Also, they are usually very experienced and either had, or currently have, a more prestigious pilot job than flight instructing.

Obviously none of this is absolute, but it tends to be the trend. Knowing whose experience level or teaching method will work best for you and your learning style may be impossible to know up front. Just remember, you can always change your flight instructor. It is not uncommon for a student, or the instructor, to decide that a particular student-teacher relationship isn't working. It should not be taken personally and there should be no hard-feelings on either side, but the decision to make a change should be executed promptly to prohibit any delays in the learning process.

For those of you fortunate enough to have your own aircraft, you will have the additional hurdle of locating an instructor that is both willing and able to give you instruction in your own airplane. There can be insurance issues which cause problems in this situation. To avoid that, you will need to seek an instructor who has experience flying your kind of aircraft. Also, many flight schools will hire their flight instructors out to you, but at a higher rate than if you were using their aircraft. This is usually due to the extra insurance they have to pay in that situation. Chalk it up to the cost of your training, and don't forget about all the money you are saving by not having to rent their airplane!

Hopefully this gives you some ammunition in making the decision on which flight school to attend, and which flight instructor to select. Just remember, no-matter where you attend, you will be learning to fly airplanes and realizing your dream of being a professional pilot!

SECTION ONE:
"TRAINING"

A Note about the FAA:

The Federal Aviation Administration (FAA) is the regulatory body of aviation in the United States. It writes and enforces all of the rules governing aviation. From mechanics to pilots, from flight schools to commercial airlines, the FAA governs it all. As a pilot they will oversee everything you do—I mean everything. This includes why, how, what, when, and where you fly with the licenses you hold. The more licensed you are, the more "freedom" (I use the term loosely) you have to fly. To be a professional pilot, you need to be rated at a minimum, as a Commercial Pilot with Instrument and Multi-Engine ratings. This section will describe in a step-by-step fashion how to accomplish that, and a little more.

- PRIVATE PILOT LICENSE -

Why?

Every professional pilot starts with their Private Pilot License. Don't let someone fool you into a Recreational Pilot or a Sport Pilot License. You don't want them because they don't apply to you. They're a waste of time and a waste of money. What you want is the Private Pilot License, often referred to simply as your "Private". And no, it is not possible to skip the Private and go straight to a higher level of licensing. Nice try though.

Getting your Private is fairly straight-forward, and arguably the easiest of the ratings to acquire—except for the hurdle of learning something completely foreign to you, but you'll get over that. This is the stage where you will be introduced to the world of flying. Along with the basic skills needed to operate an aircraft safely, you will learn theories and principles regarding weather, communication, navigation, aircraft systems, aircraft performance and aeromedical factors. But most importantly, you will begin developing your ability at aeronautical decision making. Aeronautical decision making is defined by the FAA as the "systematic approach to the mental process used by airplane pilots to consistently determine the best course of action in response to a given set of circumstances". It is the most important of your learned skills simply because it is your ability to accomplish a flight safely. It is estimated that over 75% of aircraft accidents are due in part to pilot error. Take this with the utmost seriousness, and always remember its importance. Aeronautical decision making will be a reoccurring theme throughout your entire career, and your success in this industry will depend on your ability to make sound judgments that consistently result in safe flights.

How?

The FAA has a minimum set of requirements and standards that must be met before you are able to test for your Private license. According to Federal Aviation Regulation (FAR) part 61 they are:

1. Must be at least 17 years of age.
    -If you haven't made it to your 17th birthday yet, don't worry. You can still take flight lessons at any age, and can even solo after you are 16 years old.

2. Be able to read, speak, write, and understand the English language.

    -If you can't read, speak, write, or understand the English language, then how and why are you reading this?

3. Received a logbook endorsement from an authorized instructor for the test.

    -Leave this detail to your flight instructor.

4. Have passed the required aeronautical knowledge test.

    -The aeronautical knowledge test is a written test (usually taken on a computer) that consists of multiple-choice questions covering all of the subject areas you will learn about. It is your instructor's job to make sure you are prepared for this test before he/she gives you the required endorsement in order to take it.

5. Have logged at least 40 hours of flight time that includes at least 20 hours of flight training from an authorized instructor and 10 hours of solo flight.

    -Included in these minimum time requirements are various other flight time requirements, such as 3 hours of night flying, but they are built into the total time requirement of 40 hours. These can be further explained by your instructor.

*A note regarding minimum required flight time: These minimums are exactly that, minimums. In no way does that mean you will actually complete your license in that low amount of time. To obtain your license, you absolutely must be trained to the FAA's standards, no matter how long it takes. Caveat Emptor (let the buyer beware): most flight schools will advertise a price for obtaining your Private license. These prices are almost always based on the minimum required flight time and does not account for the 25 – 100% extra flight time you will undoubtedly take to get your license. The best, most active students I have seen almost never get their license in less than 50 hours, and I would say that the norm tends to be closer to 75 hours. Plan on being somewhere in that range.

Lastly, of course, you must pass the practical test, otherwise known as the "check-ride". These tests are conducted by either an FAA examiner or a designated pilot examiner, and include both an oral and practical examination. Typically the oral portion is conducted first and consists of the examiner asking questions in a guided-discussion format. Once that is complete you both go on a flight where you demonstrate your new flying abilities. Assuming all goes well, you will walk away a newly-minted Private Pilot.

What?

So, what airplanes can I fly as a Private Pilot? Glad you asked! Initially you will be certified to fly any single-engine land airplane (SEL). Therefore, with few exceptions, you can fly any airplane with one engine that takes off and lands on terra firma (not water). In rare instances, you may obtain your Private multi-engine or seaplane licenses first, but those are typically added on later, if needed. The different airplane classifications are as follows; each requiring separate training and testing to be certified:

1. Airplane single-engine land (ASEL)
2. Airplane single-engine sea (ASES)
3. Airplane multi-engine land (AMEL)
4. Airplane multi-engine sea (AMES)

The few exceptions have to do with certain aircraft that require a small amount of training and a simple endorsement made by

an instructor in the pilot's logbook. No tests required. These
endorsements are necessary for:

1. Tail-wheel aircraft
2. Complex aircraft (retractable landing gear, flaps, and
    constant-speed propeller)
3. High Performance aircraft (more than 200 horsepower)
4. High altitude aircraft (pressurized aircraft capable of
    flight above 25,000 feet)

Additionally, any aircraft that is considered a large aircraft
(over 12,500 lbs) or is powered by a turbo-jet require what is
called a "type rating". Type ratings are aircraft specific training,
which is often intense and detailed. In other words: in order to
fly a Boeing 737, you must have a Boeing 737 type rating. And
yes, a private pilot can have a type rating for a Boeing 737—
good luck finding anyone who will actually let you fly it! In
other words, type ratings are generally not something a Private
Pilot reasonably needs.

So the answer to the question of what it is you can fly, is that
given the proper certification, endorsements, and type rating (if
necessary) a Private Pilot can fly any kind of airplane!

When and Where?

Simply put, Private Pilots can fly day or night, with or without passengers or cargo, as long as they are *not* paid for it. Other than that, the only real limitations have to do with weather. Private Pilots that are not instrument-rated are not permitted to fly into clouds or any other obstruction to visibility. The FAA has some very detailed descriptions regarding minimum weather conditions for pilots without instrument ratings—we'll get into that in the next chapter.

Additionally, Private Pilots are able to fly just about anywhere. There are certain military and government controlled airspaces that cannot be flown into, and an instrument rating is required above 18,000 feet, but other than that, the sky's the limit!

Tips for Obtaining Your Private License

- Make it clear to your instructor that you intend on being a professional pilot, and have them hold you to standards based on that goal.

- Stick to one aircraft type and avoid switching around. Aircraft can be diverse, and it takes time and effort to learn their different characteristics and limitations. This is a distraction you don't need at this point.

- Spend as much time flying solo as possible. The more time you spend alone in the airplane, the more comfortable you will be with it.

- If you have time, ask your instructor if you can sit in the back seat during other student's flights. Being able to observe others is a valuable way to reinforce what you have learned. Plus it's free instruction!

- If there is a ground-school class available, take it. This is a valuable way to reinforce what you have learned with your instructor in a class-room setting.

- Talk to your instructor and other students of the same level and attempt to combine ground lessons with them to share the cost of the instructor's time—I've never met a CFI who hasn't been receptive to this.

- Buddy-up with other students and study together. Studying together often allows you to teach each other.

Teaching someone else is one of the best ways to learn something for yourself.

- Mandatory books and publications for the Private Pilot:

  - "Pilot's Handbook of Aeronautical Knowledge." USDOT/FAA
  - "Airplane Flying Handbook." USDOT/FAA
  - "FAR/AIM (current year)." USDOT/FAA
  - "Private Pilot Single-Engine Land Practical Test Standards." USDOT/FAA
  - "Private Oral Exam Guide." USDOT/FAA
  - "Private Pilot Test Prep (current year)." ASA

- Recommended books and publications for the Private Pilot:

  - "Aviation Weather Services." USDOT/FAA
  - "Aviation Weather." FAA/NWS
  - "Aircraft Systems for Pilots." De Remer/Jeppesen
  - "Dictionary of Aeronautical Terms." Crane/ASA

- INSTRUMENT RATING -

Why?

The instrument rating is one of the most important and difficult steps in the making of a professional pilot. It is a skill that, as a professional, you will use every day of your career. So what is it, you ask? Simply put, it is a license to fly in the clouds—more accurately though, it is a license to operate by a whole different set of rules and regulations. Remember how your Private license did not allow you to fly into obstructions to visibility or above 18,000 feet? That is because the private license alone (without an instrument rating) is a license to operate under VFR (visual flight rules). Once you have become instrument rated, you are then granted the ability to operate under IFR (instrument flight rules) and thereby fly into obstructions to visibility and above 18,000 feet. IFR is the way by which all commercial airlines fly, as well as most other professional flight operations—whether there are clouds or not. Additionally, without the instrument rating, a commercial pilot is severely limited in his/her privileges as a commercial pilot (frankly, it is almost pointless to be a commercial pilot without an instrument rating, but not impossible—more on this later).

Being instrument rated however, is more than just the ability to fly under instrument flight rules. It is also the true beginning of learning to fly with precision. When an airport is reporting an overcast layer at 200 feet and visibility at ½ mile, it will take some real precision flying to line up with that runway for a landing. But you'll do it, and you'll do it safely. Remember aeronautical decision making (ADM)? We'll kick that into high gear with the instrument rating. Now you're learning to navigate without any reference to the outside—solely on instruments. You can't see the ground, you can't see the mountain next to you, and you certainly can't see other aircraft. It doesn't get much more dangerous, but IFR is a system that works, and it works because the pilots who fly by it are well trained, precision flyers who are good at their aeronautical decision making. Those who aren't usually end up killing themselves and others with them. I don't say this to scare you, but to demonstrate why the Instrument rating is one of the most important steps in becoming a professional pilot.

How?

Just like the Private license, the FAA has a set of requirements and standards that must be met in order to get your instrument rating. Here they are, according to Federal Aviation Regulation (FAR) part 61:

1. You must hold at least a current Private Pilot certificate.
   -As said before, you must start with a Private Pilot license. No skipping ahead to higher levels of certification.

2. Be able to read, speak, write, and understand the English language.
   -We covered this already. Do you understand the words on this page?

3. Received a logbook endorsement from an authorized instructor for the test.
   -Again, leave it to your instructor. This is standard procedure.

4. Have passed the required aeronautical knowledge test. -The aeronautical knowledge test is a written test (usually taken on a computer) just like you took for the Private license, only different questions. It consists of multiple-choice questions and it is your instructor's job to make sure you are prepared for this test before he/she gives you the required endorsement in order to take it.

5. Have logged at least 50 hours of cross-country flight time as pilot-in-command and a total of 40 hours of actual or simulated instrument flight. This time must include at least 15 hours of instruction from an authorized instructor. There are some other more specific flight requirements, and they can all be explained to you by your instructor.

Also, it is very important to note that up to 20 – 30 hours (depending on the situation) of the 40 hours required for instrument flight may be performed in a flight simulator or flight training device. If your flight school has a simulator or an FTD, I *highly* recommend that you take advantage of this. Flight simulators cost less than airplanes. Plus there is a pause button, which is nice because if you have a question, or do not understand something, your instructor can put the flight on hold and explain it rather than eating up ten miles in an airplane. Understand? I'm saving you money here.

And, of course, you must pass the check-ride. This will be very similar to your Private Pilot check-ride in structure, but completely different in subject. Like I said before, this one is difficult. Study, study, study, and then study some more. I failed my first attempt at the instrument rating, and now I'm a pilot for a major U.S. airline. The point is this: while failing is never fun, it can teach you things. Learn from your failures and move on. If you ever fail a check-ride, pick yourself up, dust yourself off, and immediately meet with your instructor for re-training in the area where you lacked proficiency. As long as you re-take your check-ride within 60 days, you shouldn't have to re-take the whole thing—just the part you screwed up.

What?

We've already covered what you can do as an instrument rated pilot: fly by instrument flight rules, which automatically allows you to fly in inclement weather and above 18,000 feet. But what airplanes can you fly while on instruments? The answer is: if you took the test in a single-engine airplane, you can then fly

IFR in any single-engine airplane that you are qualified to fly. If you took the test in a multi-engine airplane, you can then fly IFR in *any* airplane you are qualified to fly. The reason being, that it is typically harder to fly a multi-engine airplane than a single-engine. So if you can fly instruments in a multi-engine, then why not in a single? But, if you're following my advice, you haven't got your Multi-Engine rating yet, have you? That's next.

When and Where?

You can fly IFR anytime and anywhere. Well, not quite. There is some airspace that will still be prohibited from flight, just as previously mentioned. But generally, being able to fly IFR gives you more privilege and more ability. You can now fly in and out of weather and into the flight levels (above 18,000 feet), as long as you operate on an IFR flight plan.

Tips for Obtaining Your Instrument Rating

- Make it clear to your instructor that you intend on being a professional pilot, and have them hold you to standards based on that goal.

- If there is a ground-school class available, take it. This is a valuable way to reinforce what you have learned with your instructor in a class-room setting.

- Study hard every day. Spend lots of time studying the Federal Aviation Regulations that apply to IFR. There are a *lot* of them and the principles behind them *must* be committed to memory.

- Again, try to buddy-up and study with other students, as well as share ground school time with them, and ride in the back seat during their flights. It will save you time and money, guaranteed.

- MOST IMPORTANTLY:
  Find a good flight simulator program for your personal computer, and begin using it daily to practice what you have learned. This is not optional. Buy it and use it *every* day. I personally recommend the program "On Top" by ASA. It was designed for this exact purpose, is easy to use and doesn't have the distracting "extras" that other programs have. Doing this will save you enormous amounts of time and money in the airplane, not to mention the fact that it *will* make you a better pilot.

- Mandatory book and publications for the Instrument Pilot:

  - "FAR/AIM (current year)." USDOT/FAA
  - "Instrument Flying Handbook." USDOT/FAA
  - "Aviation Weather Services." USDOT/FAA
  - "Aviation Weather." FAA/NWS
  - "Instrument Rating Practical Test Standards." USDOT/FAA
  - "Instrument Oral Exam Guide." USDOT/FAA
  - "Instrument Test Prep (current year)." ASA
  - "Aviator's Guide to Navigation." Clausing

- Recommended books and publications for the Instrument Pilot:

  - "Instrument/Commercial Manual." Jeppesen
  - "Severe Weather Flying." Newton/ASA
  - "Aircraft Systems for Pilots." De Remer/Jeppesen
  - "Dictionary of Aeronautical Terms." Crane/ASA

- MULTI-ENGINE RATING -

Why?

Most of the professionally flown airplanes in the world have two engines or more, especially those carrying passengers. Obviously, having more engines creates more power, therefore more speed and more weight carrying ability, but the primary reason for more engines is safety. Having more than one engine means that if one fails, you will theoretically have another to fly you to safety. Additionally, having a multi-engine airplane typically means having two of every other important component. In aviation, this is referred to as redundancy. The difficulty with redundancy is that it creates twice the problems—twice the stuff to look at, to worry about, and to deal with. Not to mention that a multi-engine aircraft with one engine failed can be extremely—if not impossibly—difficult to fly. For this reason, the FAA requires that a pilot is certified to fly multi-engine airplanes before they take up a bus load of people.

How?

The Multi-Engine rating acts as a new "class" rating, meaning that it is an addendum to your current level of license. In other words, since you are already a licensed Private Pilot in single-engine land airplanes, you are now adding multi-engine land airplanes to your Private License.

There is some level of debate on the correct sequence of events in the training of a future professional pilot. Many argue that the Commercial license should come before the Multi-Engine rating, reasoning that it is one fewer check-ride (no Multi-Engine rating added to your Private license). While others, like me, believe that the Multi-Engine rating should come before the Commercial. The reason behind this is career advancement. Most pilot employers require a minimum amount of flight time in multi-engine aircraft before they will hire you. Getting the Multi-Engine rating will not alone give you this time, but by getting your Multi-Engine rating earlier in the game, you are allowing more opportunity to build this flight time, and therefore moving yourself closer to your goal of becoming a professional pilot. This principle will become more clear later, but for now, understand that by getting your Multi-Engine rating before your Commercial license will save you time, and remember: time equals money in aviation.

The FAA does not specify any minimum flight time requirements for the Multi-Engine rating, nor are you required to take an aeronautical knowledge test. The amount of time you train will be solely at the discretion of your flight instructor, and he/she will endorse your logbook once they feel you are performing to standards. This should be more incentive for you to study and perform well, so that you can cut your time and expenses.

What?

The Multi-Engine rating gives you license to operate any airplane with more than one engine that you are qualified to fly. As already stated, a class rating such as the Multi-Engine is simply an addendum to your current level of licensing.

When and Where?

If you are already instrument rated in single-engine aircraft, then your instrument rating will transfer into multi-engine aircraft as well. Plainly, your privileges will be the same as they were before, with the addition of multi-engine airplanes.

Tips for Obtaining Your Multi-Engine Rating

- As always, make it clear to your instructor that you intend on being a professional pilot, and have them hold you to standards based on that goal.

- Again, try to buddy-up and study with other students, as well as share ground school time with them and ride in the back seat during their flights.

- Put the flight simulator on your PC to use. Most flight simulators will include a multi-engine aircraft that can be programmed to randomly fail engines and other systems. This makes for excellent (and free) at-home practice.

- Mandatory books and publications for the Multi-Engine Pilot:

  - "Aircraft Systems for Pilots." De Remer/Jeppesen

- o "Private Pilot Multi-Engine Land Practical Test Standards." USDOT/FAA

- o "Multi-Engine Oral Exam Guide." USDOT/FAA

- Recommended books and publications for the Multi-Engine Pilot:

  - o "Multi-Engine Manual." Jeppesen

- COMMERCIAL LICENSE -

Why?

The answer is simple: so you can be paid to fly. The Federal Aviation Regulations state that you may not be paid, or even fully reimbursed, for your services as a pilot unless you have a Commercial Pilot's license. Therefore, until you have your commercial license, you are ineligible for any flying job that you may want to apply for. Furthermore, you cannot become a Certified Flight Instructor until you are a licensed Commercial Pilot—assuming this is a step you want to take (more on that in the next chapter).

I think it goes without saying that having your commercial license will begin to open up a lot of doors. Do I have to convince you any further?

How?

The Commercial license is going to replace your Private license. By now (if you've been following my advice) you should be a single-engine and multi-engine land Private Pilot with instrument rating. Now we will convert those ratings to your Commercial license. The instrument rating will automatically transfer, but as discussed, you will need to take two separate Commercial Pilot check-rides: one for the single-engine and another for the multi-engine. This is easier than it sounds. You will take your first check-ride in a single-engine aircraft (both cheaper and easier), which will be a full Commercial Pilot check-ride. Once this is complete you will hold a Commercial Pilot license with Single-Engine land privileges only (your Multi-Engine privileges will remain on your Private Pilot certificate). Your second test will take place in a multi-engine airplane, which should be a simple aircraft demonstration of short duration and will be more like a Multi-Engine rating check-ride than a Commercial check-ride. This is because the FAA examiner is only required to see you perform the maneuvers once. If you perform them first in a single-engine airplane, and then later that day you go for your Multi-Engine Commercial, the examiner should be happy with a short flight. That said, all FAA or designated examiners are given full authority to test or retest on whatever they deem necessary within the license and/or rating you are going for. Just don't give them a reason to test you further, right?

The maneuvers required for the Commercial license are fairly straight-forward and easy to learn. The real hurdle is building the required flight time to be eligible for the test. The following requirements are necessary to take the Commercial Pilot practical test, according to FAR part 61:

1. Must be at least 18 years old.

   -As with the private license, if you are not of age you may still train towards your Commercial. You just have to be 18 years old by the time you take the test.

2. Be able to read, speak, write, and understand the English language.

   -Are you seeing the trend?

3. Received a logbook endorsement from an authorized instructor for the test.

   -Are you seeing the other trend?

4. Have passed the required aeronautical knowledge test.
    -This test is quite involved and, as with the others, it
    should be diligently studied for. Your instructor will
    sign you off when you are ready to take it.

5. Have logged at least 250 hours of flight time which
    includes at least 100 hours of pilot-in-command (PIC)
    time and 20 hours of training towards the Commercial
    license from an authorized instructor. As with the other
    licenses/ratings, there are other flight-time requirements
    within these total times. Here are some important ones
    to note:

    a. At least 10 hours of training is required in a
        'complex' airplane. A complex airplane is one
        that has retractable landing gear, flaps, and a
        controllable pitch propeller. Unless your multi-
        engine airplane is very rare, it should also qualify
        as a complex airplane. Use it for your training,
        and you kill two birds with one stone by also
        building valuable multi-engine flight time.

    b. At least 50 hours of cross-country flight time. A
        few things to note:

i.   Whatever cross-country time you have already logged, counts towards this requirement.

ii. Your flight instructor does not need to accompany you on these flights. This will save you lots of money in the form of his/her time.

iii. With the exception of two required single-engine cross-country flights that total 4 hours, the rest should be done in a multi-engine aircraft. Here's where already having your multi-engine rating really becomes beneficial, and this is why: While it does cost more per hour, you are building much needed multi-engine flight time that will land you a job. Remember how we talked about time=money in aviation? Well here you go, by knocking out these cross-country requirements in a multi-engine airplane, you are getting this time sooner while also fulfilling a necessary requirement.

This is an invaluable concept. Believe me, I know from experience. There is nothing worse than having all the requirements for a job, except the multi-engine flight time, and not getting the job because of it. Multi-engine flight time is the hardest to get (most expensive), and you may as well get some while fulfilling other flight time requirements.

What?

Well, you should have this figured out by now, but I'll break it down for you anyhow. As a licensed Commercial Pilot, you will be able to fly any airplane that you are already rated and qualified to fly—assuming you took a Commercial check-ride in each class of airplane. We discussed how and why to do this with single-engine and multi-engine land airplanes, but what about other classes of airplane? If you had a Single-Engine or Multi-Engine Seaplane rating prior to taking your Commercial check-ride, then you will have to take additional check-rides for them to transfer to your Commercial license. Otherwise they will remain on your Private Pilot certificate. This is why, with the exception of the Multi-Engine rating, I do not recommend that future professional pilots get any additional class ratings (Single or Multi-Engine Sea) until after they are already a licensed Commercial Pilot. Once you have your Commercial license, knock yourself out. Any class rating you get thereafter will be placed directly onto your Commercial certificate. Instrument ratings and other endorsements will automatically transfer to your Commercial license. No need to worry about those.

When and Where?

Assuming you have your instrument rating, as I suggested you do, the when and where will be the same as when you finished it. A Commercial Pilot without an instrument rating is prohibited from carrying passengers for hire at night or on cross-country flights in excess of 50 nautical miles. As you can see, this is quite limiting, and I do not recommend it. There are few commercial pilot jobs where the instrument rating is not a requirement.

Tips for Obtaining Your Commercial License

- As usual, if there is a ground-school class available, then take it. This is a valuable way to reinforce what you have learned with your instructor in a class-room setting.

- As always, try to buddy-up and study with other students, as well as share ground school time with them and ride in the back seat during their flights. It will save you time and money, guaranteed.

- If you are unable to build flight time in a multi-engine airplane—do it in a tailwheel airplane. It will become clear why in a later chapter.

- Try to minimize the amount of time you spend with your instructor in airplanes and maximize the amount of time you fly solo. Your instructor's time costs money and yours doesn't. Once you have learned something from your instructor, practice it solo or even with another student who is willing to fly with you.

- Begin looking for jobs with low flight-time requirements, because you're going to want to start working as soon as you get that Commercial license.

- Mandatory books and publications:

  - "FAR/AIM (current year)." USDOT/FAA
  - "Pilot's Handbook of Aeronautical Knowledge." USDOT/FAA
  - "Airplane Flying Handbook." USDOT/FAA
  - "Commercial Pilot Single and Multi-Engine Land Practical Test Standards." USDOT/FAA
  - "Commercial Oral Exam Guide." USDOT/FAA
  - "Commercial Test Prep (current year)." ASA

- Recommended books and publications:

  - "Instrument/Commercial Manual." Jeppesen
  - "Aviation Weather Services." USDOT/FAA
  - "Aviation Weather." FAA/NWS
  - "Dictionary of Aeronautical Terms." Crane/ASA

- CERTIFIED FLIGHT INSTRUCTOR -

Why?

Being a Certified Flight Instructor (CFI) allows you to instruct other pilots towards their ratings and/or certificates. As described earlier, the basic CFI allows you to give instruction towards the Recreational, Private and Commercial licenses, as well as perform other instructor duties such as biannual flight reviews. A CFI can also, with enough experience, give instruction towards an initial CFI. To give instrument instruction, a CFI must obtain a CFII certificate, and to give multi-engine instruction, a CFI needs to also be an MEI.

The world needs flights instructors—without them we'd have no pilots—although I do not recommend becoming one if you can avoid it. Flight instruction is historically the first stepping stone into the world of professional aviation. It is the standard first job that will allow you to build your flight time for next-to-nothing pay, although employers do not necessarily look on this kind of experience as a boon. Don't get me wrong, it is an excellent time-builder that will give you enormous confidence and help to build your knowledge. The problem is that it is very difficult job that carries with it significant amounts of frustration and liability.

As a flight instructor, you are responsible for anything your student does—with or without you present. Your name and your certificate number are in their logbook, and God forbid anything happen to them or the airplane they're in, the FAA will come looking to you for answers. In some cases, you can be held responsible for your students' actions many years after you've given them instruction.

Additionally, becoming a CFI is a very difficult process that represents more time, more money, and yet another dreaded FAA check-ride. But, if you have a desire to teach and you think you'd be good at it; or you just don't have any other options, don't let me dissuade you. Flight instruction can be very rewarding, and it is probably the most readily-available first job for professional pilots.

How?

The key to becoming a CFI is finding a good CFI to teach you. The instructor who trains you to be an instructor will need to spend enormous amounts of time with you on the ground. He/she will have to cover literally every subject you have come across in aviation so far—and then some. Not only will you be clarifying the information you already know, but you will be learning how to teach it in the process. The amount of flight training towards your CFI will be minimal compared to the ground training.

FAR part 61 does not specify any minimum flight time requirements for a CFI, except that you must have logged at least 15 hours as PIC in the category and class of aircraft for the instructor rating sought. (I.E. if you want to instruct in single-engine land airplanes, you must have 15 hours PIC in single-engine land airplanes). There is however, a substantial list of maneuvers and procedures that you must be trained and *instructionally* proficient in to become a CFI. It will take significant time and effort. Here are the rest of the CFI requirements:

1. Be at least 18 years old.

2. Be able to read, speak, write, and understand the English language.

3. Received *multiple* logbook endorsements from an authorized instructor.

4. Pass a knowledge test on the Fundamentals of Instruction.
    Waived if you are already a certified flight or ground instructor or if you hold a current teacher's certificate or are employed as a teacher at a college or university.

5. Have passed the required aeronautical knowledge test.

What?

As a CFI, you will be rated to teach in single-engine land airplanes. If you wanted to teach in single-engine sea airplanes, all you would need is a single-engine seaplane rating on your Commercial certificate and 15 hours as PIC. To instruct in Multi-Engine airplanes however, requires a separate instructor certificate, referred to as the MEI. As an MEI, you are required to have at least 5 hours of PIC in make and model of multi-engine aircraft to give instruction. All instructors must first become a CFI though.

When and Where?

Your when and where privileges do not change as a flight instructor. In fact, although you are required to be a CFII to instruct IFR students, a CFI without a CFII may still give students training in poor weather as long as it is not training towards the Instrument rating. Additionally, flight instructors may not give more than 8 hours of flight instruction in a consecutive 24-hour period.

Tips for becoming a Certified Flight Instructor

- Definitely take a ground-school class if available. Especially any class that teaches the 'Fundamentals of Instruction'.

- Absolutely get a group of other CFI candidates together to do ground school with. Your CFI should have no problem with getting 3 or 4 of you together in a classroom to save time.

- Study your butt off. Becoming a CFI is the most study-intensive of all the licenses and ratings. Don't skimp a bit.

- Make your own binder of lesson plans on every subject. This is a time and labor intensive process, but it will solidify what you are learning and give you an excellent reference to look back on.

- Once you are a CFI, don't waste any time in becoming a CFII and/or MEI. This will give you more marketability and therefore more students.

- Mandatory books and publications:

  - "FAR/AIM (current year)." USDOT/FAA
  - "Pilot's Handbook of Aeronautical Knowledge." USDOT/FAA
  - "Airplane Flying Handbook." USDOT/FAA
  - "Aviation Instructor's Handbook." USDOT/FAA
  - "Flight Instructor Single-Engine Practical Test Standards." USDOT/FAA
  - "Certified Flight Instructor Oral Exam Guide." USDOT/FAA

- ○ "Certified Flight Instructor Test Prep." ASA

- Recommended books and publications:

  - ○ Everything. At this point there is nothing you shouldn't be sticking your nose in. I recommend at least one full shelf packed with books as reference material.

- AIRLINE TRANSPORT PILOT -

The Air Transport Pilot (ATP) license is the last and ultimate license. It is essentially the replacement for your Commercial licenses, and is the certification which allows you to be the pilot-in-command (i.e. captain) for most airlines or charter operations. In addition to other requirements, you must have logged a minimum of 1,500 flight hours to become an ATP (in other words, significant experience). By the time you have that kind of experience, you will realize that most employers will usually train you towards, and pay for your ATP. Moral of the story: except for specific and special circumstances, do not get your ATP on your own. It's a waste of time and money that way.

What you should do, is begin to study for your ATP written once you are already a licensed Commercial Pilot. You do not need an endorsement to take the ATP written, nor do you need to be actively training for it—you can do it at your own discretion. However, the ATP written is by far the most difficult and comprehensive written exam there is. In it, there will be many foreign subjects to you. Obtain a copy of the ATP study guide, and live with it for several months prior to taking the test. I cannot over-emphasize how much studying this demands.

Most employers either require, or like to see that you have taken the ATP written test. Even so, it makes a great resume addition, and your results don't expire for two years, unless you are employed at an airline—then they don't expire at all. But even if you don't actually take the test, begin to study for it, because eventually you will have to—and it's tough!

SECTION TWO:

"PAYING YOUR DUES"

The granting of a license is merely the first check upon his ability. Throughout his career he will be called upon to demonstrate to hard-bitten examiners his awareness of the latest regulations and his continuing ability to do his job at the highest standard. His performance during the twice-yearly simulator checks will be analysed no less critically that that of an actor playing his first Hamlet. If he survives, he prays that the doctors will pass him fit on his regular medical check. In return he will get a smart uniform, a great fillip to his self-esteem, an image in society, a good salary and the opportunity to sit up all night hunched over the aircraft controls in a cramped flight deck.

Few people meet the criteria demanded. Pilots are required to be averagely good at all things. Eliminate from the population at large all those who require spectacles, those suffering from minor medical conditions like colour blindness, young men who never went on to further education, those who couldn't steer a tram down a Roman road without hitting a tree, and the people who quite sensibly insist upon sleeping in their own bed at night, and there are precious few left to choose from.

- David Beaty[†]

[†]Beaty, David. The Naked Pilot. Shrewsbury, England: Airlife, 2001.

- FIRST JOB -

Why?

You're at the bottom, and you've got to start somewhere. You desperately need to continue putting flight time in your logbook, but just can't afford or justify paying for it anymore. You want to start getting paid to fly, and to stop having to pay to fly. It's an amazing feeling the first time you go up and fly an airplane, and someone pays *you* to do it! But this first job is not about the money. No, the money will be a pittance—trust me. Your first job is all about the flight time. As a professional pilot, nothing will get your foot in the door better than your logbook. Your logbook, in essence, is your resume. The more flight time you have in your logbook, the more experienced you are as a pilot. Your first job, hopefully, will be your time-builder. You will most likely be entering the job market as a newly-minted commercial pilot with very little flight time. The job choices will be limited, but no matter what you do, look for the one that will best boost your proverbial resume: flight hours.

What?

Just as important as the amount of flight time in your logbook, is the *kind* of flight time in your logbook. Most "first jobs" will gladly put you in command of a single-engine Cessna, but none will put you in any seat of a Boeing 747. This is because to fly an aircraft such as the Boeing 747, you need to have prior experience in turbine powered aircraft. Turbine flight time, especially multi-engine turbine flight time, is the most important kind of flight time that you can have in your logbook—and the more of it the better. Read my words: leave the piston aircraft on the ramp, and don't be afraid to sell your soul for turbine flight time. Getting turbine flight time, however, is much easier said than done. So if you can't get it out of the gates, then do everything you can to fly multi-engine airplanes. It's the next best thing. Remember that most professionally flown aircraft are multi-engines? Well, just as with turbine aircraft, it is impossible to get a job without some decent level of multi-engine experience. This is the exact reason why I recommend knocking some of this time out during your commercial training (this was previously discussed in detail, if you don't remember then go back and read it).

And finally, if you aren't able to get some quality time in multi-engine aircraft, then get as much diverse flight time in single-engine aircraft as you can. I mean tail-wheel, seaplane, whatever. Just get it no matter what. There are few pilots that don't have heaps of single-engine flight time—it's your job to stand out from the rest. As I said: don't be afraid to sell your soul for flight time. Suffer for it. Move wherever you have to, work for as little as you have to, and do anything you have to. Just get the flight time. Whatever personal suffering you experience will be temporary. Very temporary. There is a big difference between the marketability of a commercial pilot with 300 hours of total time and the marketability of a commercial pilot with 1000 hours of total time—and it can take less than a year to get from one to the other.

How?

The following are descriptions of some common "first jobs" that will help you to build your flight time:

- <u>Flight Instruction</u>
  A lot has already been said about flight instruction, but just to re-iterate:

While flight instruction is probably the most common first job for the aspiring professional pilot, I do not recommend it if you can avoid it. That's not to mean flight instruction is a bad job—it's not. It can be exceptionally rewarding and quite a confidence builder, but it is also an extreme liability.

Flight instruction will typically build your total flight time very quickly. It is not uncommon for ambitious flight instructors at busy flight schools to log 1000 flight hours per year. What it will not do, is build your turbine time. How can you teach in a turbine airplane when you have no experience in one yourself? You can't, and you won't. Yeah, you might get lucky and find a flight school with a charter department that wants you to fly right seat in their jet on charter flights, but these jobs are *rare*. Don't count on it, even if it is suggested to you in an interview. Often, your low flight time will prohibit you from qualifying on their insurance anyhow.

All this said: don't let me discourage you from flight instruction if it is all you can get. It is the most common path and there is nothing about it that will be seen negatively by a prospective employer. It is a noble and respectable first job.

- Tow Pilot

  Remember back when you were getting your Private
  license, and I recommended that you try to get it in a
  tail-wheel airplane if at all possible? And then when you
  were getting your Commercial license, I recommended
  that if you were not able to build time in a multi-engine
  airplane that you should do it in a tail-wheel? Having the
  option to work as a tow pilot is the reason why.

  Unfortunately, tail-wheel aircraft are becoming a thing
  of the past, and the pilots who fly them are too. Most
  tail-wheel aircraft still in existence are relics operated by
  their owners for pleasure, and licensed commercial
  pilots who are both qualified and willing to fly a tail-
  wheel are hard to find. With few exceptions, the only
  common tail-wheel jobs either involve towing a banner
  or towing a glider. Most tail-wheel jobs require at least
  100 hours of tail-wheel flight time. Since you took my
  advice, and built tail-wheel time during your training,
  you are now eligible for these jobs—and you shouldn't
  have any problem getting one since there are so few
  qualified pilots.

Whether you're towing banners or towing gliders, its great time-building experience. You'll get to spend lots of time flying by yourself, building your skills and becoming a better pilot. However, as with flight instruction, it is probably not multi-engine and it is definitely not turbine flight time. But none-the-less, it is a job, and it puts the hours in your logbook.

- Traffic Watch/Pipeline Patrol
  These two jobs are both very similar in that they require you to monitor events from an aircraft. Traffic watch pilots will generally fly twice a day: first during morning traffic and last during evening traffic. Pipeline patrol generally involves flying over pipelines to monitor their condition.
  Both jobs will almost always be in single-engine piston airplanes. But they almost always have no minimum flight time requirements, and again, are good time-building jobs. They also make a great addendum to your flight instructing job.

- Skydive Pilot
  This job you may or may not qualify for, depending on the operation. There are various types of aircraft being

operated to fly skydivers, in both single-pilot and multi-crew environments. Many of them, especially nowadays, are turbine powered. The right operation will have both piston-singles and turbine airplanes, so that you could start in the piston and work up with experience to the turbine.

Flying skydivers can be exhilarating, and can provide the much desired turbine flight time experience, but it is typically not the best time-building job. Most skydive pilots don't actually log a lot of flight time compared to other commercial pilots. This is because skydive businesses can't make money unless that airplane gets up to altitude as quick as possible, drops their divers, and gets back on the ground before they do.

- Part 135 Pilot
Part 135 generally refers to cargo operations, or possibly flying passengers for charter. Out of all the first jobs, *this* is the one you want to look for. Almost nothing is better than a first job flying from point to point in good and bad weather, delivering goods or people. And these jobs are almost always done in turbine-powered or at least multi-engine airplanes.

As pilot-in-command, you will need at least 500 hours total-time to fly as a VFR only part 135 pilot. Regardless of what anyone tells you, these jobs do exist—they just usually are not advertised. I recommend going to all the cargo operations you know of and ask them if they have spots available. But the more readily available job will be a co-pilot position. They usually don't pay squat, and they will abuse your personal time, but you will log valuable flight time and gain part 135 experience that is highly regarded by the airlines.

- Part 121 Pilot

 Part 121 means an airline. These jobs, for inexperienced pilots, are far and few between—but they do exist. If you can get one, it is a better job than part 135 jobs. You will most definitely be flying turbine powered, multi-engine airplanes and you will probably fly a lot of hours. The problem is getting the job. You'll probably have to look to the ends of the earth, or at least the continent, but you'll find them—usually in Alaska. This is because it's hard to get people to come to work up there. Like I said, don't be afraid to sacrifice. All it takes is one year at a job like this and you've paved your future.

When and Where?

The when is now! Time is money, remember? You shouldn't waste even a second looking for your first job as a pilot, and don't be too picky. Take what comes at you; it's really all the same: you'll be putting experience, in the form of flight time, in your logbook. And that is priceless.

Where are these jobs? The answer is they're everywhere. This is why you have to be willing to sacrifice. Remember that the sacrifice is temporary, and by making it you are investing in a big future, that pays high rewards. But don't fret if you can't get the 121 job out of the gates, there's another airline around the corner that is waiting to give you a job—they just want to see some experience first. So pull up your bootstraps and get the flight time in your logbook, next up is the regional airlines.

Tips for Getting Your First Job:

- Flight schools are generally desperate for new instructors. Apply at all the local schools, and maybe some more distant ones. Always keep in mind which one will get you the most flight time.

- Climbto350 (www.climbto350.com) is an excellent resource for locating and researching aviation jobs. Multiple job listings from around the world are posted by employers everyday. There is a small fee to view the listings, however it is money well spent.

- Don't be afraid to apply for jobs that you may not have the "minimum flight time" for. Often these employers are simply fishing for more of an experienced pilot than they can afford.

- Whenever possible, apply in person. It has become almost common-place for pilots to send their resumes to prospective employers via email. From my own experience, it is far easier to get a job if you can present your resume in person. Put a face to the name, so-to-speak.

- Mandatory reading:

"The Turbine Pilot's Flight Manual." Brown/Holt

- THE REGIONALS -

Why?

At some point, you're going to start getting really bored of teaching stalls all day in a crappy single-engine Cessna, or flying the same stretch of highway, reporting traffic. You're going to want a taste of the real thing. It won't take long for you to get really tired of that first job, and want to start flying jets all over the country with good-looking flight attendants in the back.

The regional airlines are typically the next step in the professional pilot's career. As a general rule, to begin applying you'll need around 1000 hours of total time and 100 hours of multi-engine time. Regional airlines usually hire pilots regardless of their previous turbine experience, so if you haven't gotten any by now, this is your chance. There are no pistons here—it's all multi-engine turbines, so no more worrying about that. But what's more, is that you will be working in a multi-crew environment (more than one pilot, plus flight attendants). Many employers have begun to require that you have some experience in a multi-crew environment before you can apply with them. Almost all jet aircraft and most large turbo-prop aircraft require at least two pilots, and possibly a flight engineer. Working in this kind of environment can be difficult if you are not used to it, but it is necessary for safety of flight considerations.

What?

Almost all regional airlines have begun operating small passenger jets, referred to as the regional jet, or RJ. Additionally, most regional airlines operate fleets of large transport-category turbo-props. Regardless of the aircraft you're hired to fly, you'll probably have the opportunity to fly them all eventually, if you want.

What's important is not the aircraft you fly, but upgrading to captain as soon as possible. Now that you've made it this far, it is extremely important that you start logging multi-engine turbine PIC time. You can't do that until you're a captain. When I first started flying as a First Officer for a regional airline, growth was explosive in the aviation industry. Pilots were upgrading to captain in as little as 8 months from the day they were hired. As I sit here and write, there is absolutely no movement. No-one is becoming a captain, and no-one is leaving for major airlines. It could be years before the movement begins again. It's all market timing, which you cannot control.

But you'll need at least 1000 hours as PIC before you can take the next step in your career, so focus on doing what you have to in order to upgrade. From where you sit, nothing should be more important—and don't be afraid to bend over backwards to make it happen. The quicker you do, the sooner you can move on to bigger and better things.

How?

As I said before, most regional airlines will begin accepting your application when you have logged a minimum of 1000 hours of total time and 100 hours of multi-engine time. Of course, it can vary a little from airline to airline. Be sure to check their websites for their current requirements. You can usually fill out an electronic application on their website, and typically this is all it takes to get the interview. If the airline you are applying for has group interviews scheduled, I recommend attending one. It is basically a way to interview without being invited.

Getting the interview is the easy part. Passing the interview and being offered the job is something entirely different. Interviews are different, depending on the airline, but most follow a similar process which consists of these elements, in no particular order:

1. Written test
2. Human resources interview
3. Technical interview
4. Simulator evaluation

To prepare, I highly recommend studying interview "gouges", if available. These are other people's accounts of their interview experience, which generally included specific questions asked of them. These gouges are usually found on the internet quite easily, but it is better if you can get them from friends who have interviewed at the airline themselves—this helps ensure accuracy. In addition to the gouges, I *highly* recommend that you get some practice time in a simulator of the same model that the airline you are interviewing with has (if possible). At a minimum, practice your heart-out on your PC simulator. A lot of interviews are failed in the simulator. It's your only chance to show them that you can actually fly. Also, if possible, try to schedule multiple interviews within the same time period, with your last choice airline first and your first choice airline last.

This way you will be well versed in the interview experience by the time you interview at your airline of choice, and who knows, maybe you'll get offered multiple jobs and have your pick.

Don't underestimate the value of interview preparation. Treat it like it is your biggest check-ride ever. Study very hard and use every resource available to you. Every subject is fair game in the airline interview, so don't skimp. And lastly, if you don't get offered the job, re-apply and try again. Airlines seem to like this. It shows determination, and a willingness to improve. I personally know people who have interviewed as much as three times before they got the job. Moral of the story: never give up.

When and Where?

There are quite a few regional airlines out there, and each one is unique to itself. While the most important step is actually getting the job, how do you decide which ones to apply to? And, assuming you get multiple offers, which job to take? Here are some key things to consider, in order of importance:

1. How long until I can upgrade to captain?

   -We discussed the importance of this. Obviously you want as short as possible amount of time.

2. How stable is the company? What are my chances of being furloughed?

   -Furloughs are not uncommon in the aviation industry. They are not good—it basically means you are on the street without a job because your company can't afford to pay you any longer. I know people who have been furloughed as many as three times in a single decade.

3. What domiciles do they have?

   -Hopefully they have a domicile that is close to your home. If not, are their domiciles in places that you can afford to live for the pittance they'll pay you?

4. How is the pay?

   -Notice how this is last on the list. This is because regional airlines tend to pay similarly—and it won't be much. But you're not in it for the money, right?

Hopefully by now you have some friends working for some of these regional airlines and you can pick their brains about their respective companies. Friends are also really good for helping you get jobs. Inside recommendations tend to be highly regarded in the airline business, so start hitting your friends up with requests for letters of recommendation. If you don't have any friends at any airlines, then there is quite a bit of information available on the internet, including some wildly popular forums where you can chat with airline pilots. Use this as a resource to ask any questions you may have. I see this all the time, and it is quite effective.

Tips for Getting Jobs with Regional Airlines

- Use Airline Pilot Central (www.airlinepilotcentral.com) to research different airlines. This is a phenomenal website that is dedicated to maintaining up-to-date hiring information and pay scales for most airlines.

- Also use the extensive aviation forums at Airline Pilot Central to research, discuss, and ask questions about different airlines.

- Visit www.aviationinterviews.com for a substantial and comprehensive collection of interview gouges, and don't forget to submit your own once you have been interviewed.

- Mandatory reading:

"Airline Pilot Technical Interviews: A Study Guide."
McElroy, Ronald D

- OTHER OPPROTUNITIES -

Once you have some time under your belt and have started to wear-out your first job, some other opportunities may begin to arise that aren't in the regional airline category. These opportunities are various, and there is no way we could dissect them all here in this guide. However, here is an example of an opportunity a friend of mine had, and how it ensued:

> After a couple of years working hard as a flight instructor, Jason had built up enough hours to begin applying at some regional airlines. He wasn't sure it was what he wanted to do, but after much encouragement from his friends, he began submitting applications. After a couple months went by Jason, who was becoming burnt-out with flight instructing and desperate to find a new job, still hadn't gotten any invitations to interview with an airline. Then one day a wealthy flight student of Jason's approached him with a job opportunity: his company had just purchased a brand-new Beechcraft King Air for their much needed business travel

purposes, and would Jason like to come on board as their pilot? He could expect to fly all day, five days a week, but would be home every night and be well-compensated for it. Jason's problems were solved! Not only did he have a new job, but he would be piloting a brand-new multi-engine turbine aircraft!

That same day however, the regional airline of Jason's choice called and asked him to come in for an interview in a couple days. Without anything to lose, he agreed and decided to interview just for the experience. The interview went well, and he was glad he did it. The people at the airline were nice, and it gave him a good idea of what the airline interview process was like.

The next day, the day before he was to start training in his new King Air, the airline called Jason and gave him the job, with class starting the following week. What to do? Jason now had two job opportunities, and a choice needed to be made. On one hand he could take the job flying the King Air and make really good money, logging PIC turbine flight time; on the other hand he could take the airline job for little money, but with great opportunity for career advancement. After much deliberation, Jason decided to turn down the corporate job and accept the position at the airline. His friend

Mike, who had the same experience and qualifications, would fill his position at the wealthy student's company. A couple of years later, all was well with Jason. He had made captain at the airline within his first year, and was now making as much money as he would have had he stuck with the corporate job. He had logged well over 1000 hours of turbine PIC time and was beginning to apply at major airlines.

His friend Mike however, was not so fortunate. After a couple of years, things seemed to be going well. He was well compensated and like Jason, had logged over 2000 hours of PIC turbine flight time. However, the business he worked for was not doing so well, and he just received notice that they were declaring bankruptcy. Within a week, Mike was on the street without a job. So, he called Jason, who had just been hired at a major airline to see if he could get a job there—after all, he had twice the PIC turbine time that Jason had. So Jason took Mike's resume and handed it to his chief pilot. After briefly reviewing it, the chief pilot denied an interview for Mike because he didn't have any part 121 experience or any flight time in a crew environment.

Without any other options, Mike took a job at the same regional airline that Jason had started at a couple years prior. He did this so that he could build his experience in at a part 121 airline, and hopefully qualify to work at a major airline someday in the future.

This is a true story based on the experiences of my friends. Initially it seemed as though Jason had taken a real gamble with his career, while Mike had taken the sure road. As things materialized, however, it became clear that Jason's decision, while sacrificial in terms of compensation, turned out wiser. Mike didn't necessarily make a bad decision—he still has a logbook full of valuable experience that he was well compensated for—but unfortunately he put himself right back where he had started a couple years prior.

The moral of the story is this: while many different opportunities may come your way after that fist job, each one needs to be looked at very carefully. There are benefits to each opportunity, but the ramifications may not be felt until many years down the road. It all depends on what you ultimately want in your career. Jason and Mike's story could have gone differently. Jason could have been furloughed before he ever made captain, while Mike's company could have expanded and bought more airplanes, hiring more pilots.

There is one thing that is for sure though, and that is that the regional airline experience cannot hurt you. No matter what your ultimate career goals in aviation are, working for a regional airline is an excellent step that gives you a well-rounded experience. You will put meaningful flight time in your logbook that will be regarded as quality by future employers. I strongly recommend looking hard at every opportunity that comes your way, and asking yourself: Is this an experience that will equal that of the regional airlines, regardless of pay or benefits? If the answer is no, and an airline job is available to you, then walk away.

SECTION THREE:

"REALIZING THE DREAM"

- MAJOR AIRLINE PILOT -

Why?

Many professional pilots don't ever move on to the "major" airlines because they get used to their quality of life. You see, in the airline business, seniority is everything. It dictates your pay, your schedule, where you live, etc. Once you have put in some time at a regional airline, you will begin to realize the value of having a little seniority. While your pay may never be as good as it could be at the major airlines, your schedule can, and probably will be better at the regional level. There is something to be said for quality of life…

But for those of you who have their eyes on the prize, the major airlines will provide you with substantially more compensation, and will give you the opportunity to fly bigger, dare I say, "badder" airplanes. Unfortunately, you will start-over at the bottom of the seniority list—but who cares when you're making six figures, right?

What?

I assume you've got this one figured out. But for those of you who are a little slow: If you've ever wanted to fly some of the biggest, most powerful airplanes on the planet. The major airlines are the place to do it.

How?

Getting a job at a major airline will be a very similar experience to getting a job at the regional level. Refer back to that chapter if need be. The biggest difference now will be getting your foot in the door. Major airlines traditionally rely heavily on internal recommendations, so it's a very good idea to network and make lots of friends during your time in the regional airlines. These contacts will one day be your source for letters of recommendation.

In addition to knowing the right people, you will have to have the experience. Minimum flight time requirements vary from airline to airline, and can change depending on needs. However, generally speaking, you can begin applying to major airlines once you have logged at least 1000 hours of PIC multi-engine turbine time. See why I place so much importance on this kind of flight time? It is everything in regards to experience when you get to the top.

Most airlines will also require that you have at least 1500 hours of total flight time and be licensed as an ATP, but this shouldn't be a problem, especially if you are coming from a regional airline. In addition, many airlines are beginning to require at least 1000 hours of flight time in a multi-crew environment. So if you've been flying around single-pilot, time to find yourself a job in the right seat somewhere.

When and Where?

Deciding on which airline you want to work for is simply a matter of preference. Many people will look at pay more seriously; others look at domicile options as the deciding factor. My personal opinion is that you should base your decision on the stability of the airline. The airline industry is extremely moody, and the large swings in stability will definitely affect the pilot group. It is not uncommon to hear of a seasoned airline pilot who has been furloughed (possibly more than once), only to concede to pay-cuts just to get his job back. Similarly, it is not uncommon for airlines to file bankruptcy or completely go out of business. Wisely choosing the airline you want to work for is the best thing you can do for yourself. Don't make the mistake of jumping into the first job that comes your way just because they have big and cool airplanes. Hold out for the companies that you think are going to weather the storm well, and you'll be glad you did. Accepting a job at XYZ airline because they pay more doesn't really make sense when two years later they'll put you on the street.

The other thing to keep in mind is that if you don't like where you're at once you get the major airline job, it is very difficult to jump ship. Remember that seniority is everything and that whatever seniority you've worked up to will not transfer with you when you leave. If you leave one company for another, regardless of your experience, you will start over at the bottom. This holds true for regional airlines as well. So, take the decision to switch companies with a large dose of consequence, and avoid being in that position at all by picking your airline wisely.

Tips for Getting Jobs with Major Airlines

- Use Airline Pilot Central (www.airlinepilotcentral.com) to research different airlines. This is a phenomenal website that is dedicated to maintaining up-to-date hiring information and pay scales for most airlines, both regional and major.

- Also use the extensive aviation forums at Airline Pilot Central to research, discuss, and ask questions about different airlines.

- Visit www.aviationinterviews.com for a substantial and comprehensive collection of interview gouges, and don't forget to submit your own once you have interviewed.

- Mandatory book::

"Airline Pilot Technical Interviews: A Study Guide." McElroy, Ronald D

- FINAL WORD -

"Flying is a hard way to earn an easy living"

I don't know who said that phrase, but it is my favorite aviation truth. Becoming a professional pilot isn't easy—never was, never will be. But once you're there, it's the easiest money you'll ever make, because it's fun and you enjoy it…and that's the key: to have fun. If you aren't having fun, then you shouldn't be doing it. It's too costly—financially and otherwise—if you aren't enjoying it. I've personally witnessed people make this error, and it always ends in disappointment and failure. I beg you, don't make that mistake.

But for those of you who are having fun and are truly enjoying the thrill of flying airplanes, keep at it. There will be times of frustration and difficulty—that's the hard part. But the rewards are incomparable, and worth pursuing. I trust this guide is helpful in achieving your goals in professional aviation. It is a wonderful career that I hope you have the opportunity to experience. My
hat goes off to you if you do. I've been there myself, and I know what it takes and what you'll go through to get there.

Best of Luck!

CPSIA information can be obtained at www.ICGtesting.com
Printed in the USA
BVOW02s2011100615

404048BV00002B/511/P

9 780578 034386